Grade 1 Ages 6–7

WITHDRAWN

Master Math at Home

Exploring Multiplication and Division

Scan the QR code to help your child's learning at home.

 |

mastermathathome.com

ROCKFORD PUBLIC LIBRARY

How to use this book

Math — No Problem! created **Master Math at Home** to help children develop fluency in the subject and a rich understanding of core concepts.

Key features of the Master Math at Home books include:

- Carefully designed lessons that provide structure, but also allow flexibility in how they're used. For example, some children may want to write numbers, while others might want to trace.

- Speech bubbles containing content designed to spark diverse conversations, with many discussion points that don't have obvious "right" or "wrong" answers.

- Rich illustrations that will guide children to a discussion of shapes and units of measurement, allowing them to make connections to the wider world around them.

- Exercises that allow a flexible approach and can be adapted to suit any child's cognitive or functional ability.

- Clearly laid-out pages that encourage children to practice a range of higher-order skills.

- A community of friendly and relatable characters who introduce each lesson and come along as your child progresses through the series.

You can see more guidance on how to use these books at mastermathathome.com.

We're excited to share all the ways you can learn math!

Copyright © 2022 Math — No Problem!

Math — No Problem!
mastermathathome.com
www.mathnoproblem.com
hello@mathnoproblem.com

First American Edition, 2022
Published in the United States by DK Publishing
1745 Broadway, 20th Floor, New York, NY 10019

22 23 24 25 26 10 9 8 7 6 5 4 3 2 1
002–327120–Nov/2022

This book was made with Forest Stewardship Council™ certified paper—one small step in DK's commitment to a sustainable future. For more information go to www.dk.com/our-green-pledge

All rights reserved. Without limiting the rights under the copyright reserved above, no part of this publication may be reproduced, stored in or introduced into a retrieval system, or transmitted, in any form, or by any means (electronic, mechanical, photocopying, recording, or otherwise), without the prior written permission of the copyright owner.
Published in Great Britain by Dorling Kindersley Limited

A catalog record for this book is available from the Library of Congress.

ISBN: 978-0-7440-5180-3
Printed and bound in China

For the curious
www.dk.com

Acknowledgments

The publisher would like to thank the authors and consultants Andy Psarianos, Judy Hornigold, Adam Gifford, Dr. Wong Khoon Yoong, and Dr. Anne Hermanson.

The Castledown typeface has been used with permission from the Colophon Foundry.

Contents

	Page
Groups	4
Multiplying by 2	6
Multiplying by 5	8
Multiplying by 10	10
More Multiplying	12
Word Problems	16
Grouping	18
Sharing	20
Dividing by 2	22
Dividing by 5	24
Dividing by 10	26
Multiplication and Division	28
More Word Problems	30
Review and Challenge	36
Answers	46

Ruby   Elliott   Amira   Charles   Lulu   Sam   Oak   Holly   Ravi   Emma   Jacob   Hannah

Groups

Starter

How many children are there on the teacup ride?

Example

3 + 3 + 3 + 3 = 12

There are 4 teacups on the ride. Each teacup has 3 children. There are 4 threes.

4 × 3 = 12
We say 4 times 3 equals 12.

There are 12 children on the teacup ride.

Practice

Fill in the blanks.

1

☐ + ☐ + ☐ = ☐

☐ groups of ☐ = ☐

☐ × ☐ = ☐

2

☐ + ☐ + ☐ + ☐ + ☐ + ☐ = ☐

☐ groups of ☐ = ☐

☐ × ☐ = ☐

Multiplying by 2

Lesson 2

Starter

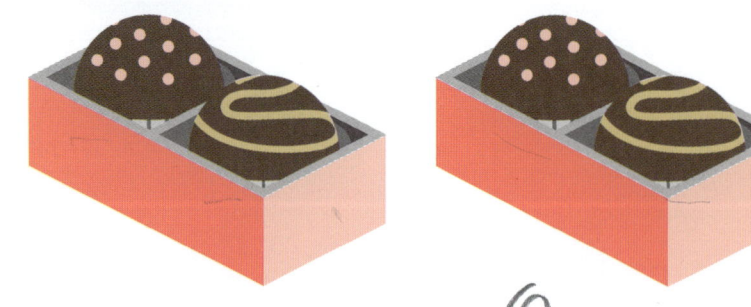

How many chocolates are there? 0

Example

1 box of 2 chocolates   1 box of 2 chocolates   1 box of 2 chocolates

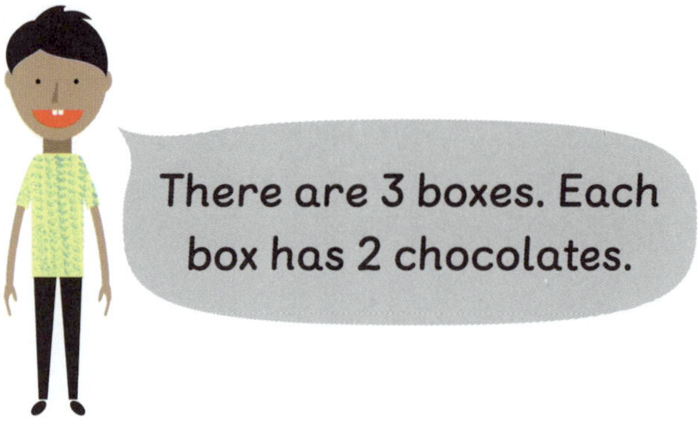

There are 3 boxes. Each box has 2 chocolates.

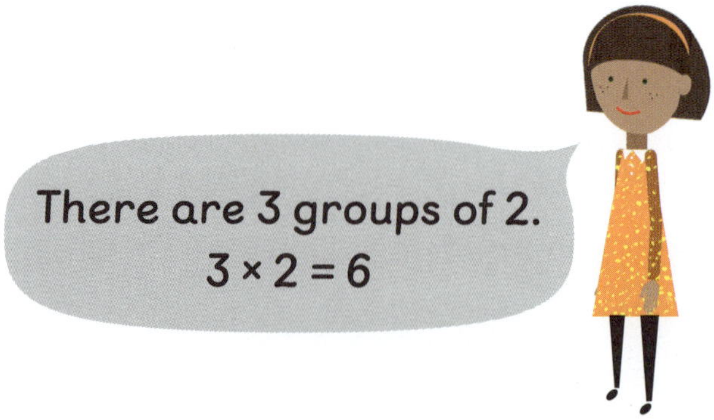

There are 3 groups of 2.
3 × 2 = 6

There are 6 chocolates.

6

Practice

Fill in the blanks.

1 group of 2 = 2
1 × 2 = 2

2 groups of 2 = 4

| 4 | × | 3 | = | 12 |

| 4 | groups of | 4 | = | 10 |

☐ × ☐ = ☐

☐ groups of ☐ = ☐
☐ × ☐ = ☐

☐ groups of ☐ = ☐
☐ × ☐ = ☐

☐ groups of ☐ = ☐
☐ × ☐ = ☐

☐ groups of ☐ = ☐
☐ × ☐ = ☐

☐ groups of ☐ = ☐
☐ × ☐ = ☐

☐ groups of ☐ = ☐
☐ × ☐ = ☐

☐ groups of ☐ = ☐
☐ × ☐ = ☐

7

Multiplying by 5

Lesson 3

Starter

How many hot dogs did Charles make for the party?

Example

1	2	3	4	5	6	7	8	9	10
11	12	13	14	15	16	17	18	19	20
21	22	23	24	25	26	27	28	29	30

I can count in fives using the number chart.

Can you see a pattern in the number chart?

There are 6 fives.
6 × 5 = 30
Charles made 30 hot dogs for the party.

Practice

Count the stickers and fill in the blanks.

1 group of 5 = 5
1 × 5 = 5

2 groups of 5 = 10
☐ × ☐ = ☐

☐ groups of ☐ = ☐
☐ × ☐ = ☐

☐ groups of ☐ = ☐
☐ × ☐ = ☐

☐ groups of ☐ = ☐
☐ × ☐ = ☐

☐ groups of ☐ = ☐
☐ × ☐ = ☐

☐ groups of ☐ = ☐
☐ × ☐ = ☐

☐ groups of ☐ = ☐
☐ × ☐ = ☐

☐ groups of ☐ = ☐
☐ × ☐ = ☐

☐ groups of ☐ = ☐
☐ × ☐ = ☐

Multiplying by 10

Lesson 4

Starter

How many crayons are there on the table?

Example

There are 6 boxes.
Each box has 10 crayons.
6 × 10 = 60

There are 60 crayons on the table.

Practice

1 Count and fill in the blanks.

(a)

☐ groups of ☐ = ☐

☐ × 10 = ☐

(b)

☐ groups of ☐ = ☐

☐ × ☐ = ☐

(c)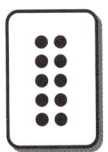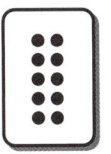

☐ groups of ☐ = ☐

☐ × ☐ = ☐

2 Fill in the blanks.

(a) 2 × 10 = ☐

(b) 6 × 10 = ☐

(c) 5 × 10 = ☐

(d) 10 × 10 = ☐

More Multiplying

Lesson 5

Starter

How can we work out how many stickers there are?

Example

There are
2 groups of 10 stickers.
2 × 10 = 20
There are 20 stickers.

There are
10 groups of 2 stickers.
10 × 2 = 20
I agree, there are
20 stickers.

2 × 10 = 10 × 2
They are both
equal to 20.

5 × 4 = 4 × 5
They are also both equal to 20.

Practice

1 Fill in the blanks.

(a)

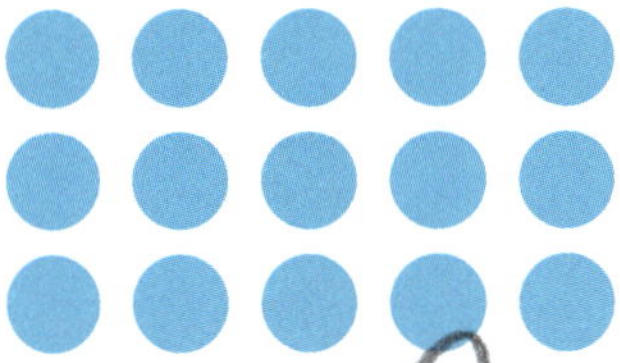

5 × ☐ 10 = mow   ☐ × 5

5 × ☐ = 15

☐ × 5 = 15

(b) 2 × 4 = 4 × 2

2 × ☐ = ☐

☐ × 2 = ☐

(c)

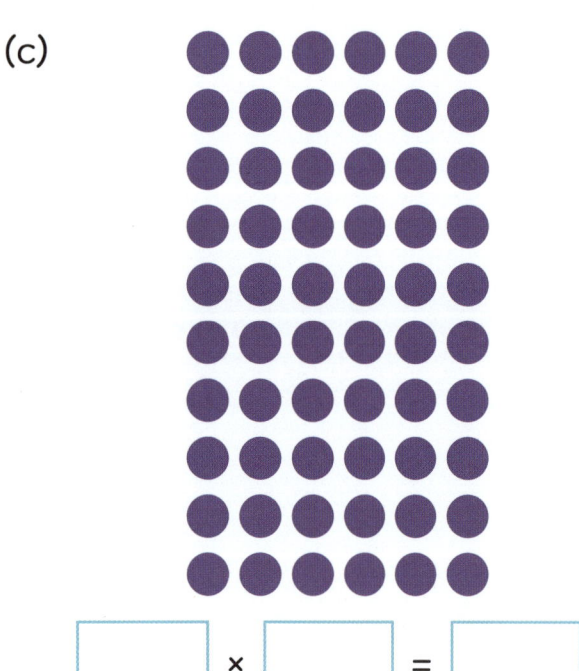

☐ × ☐ = ☐   ☐ × ☐ = ☐

2 Draw lines to match.

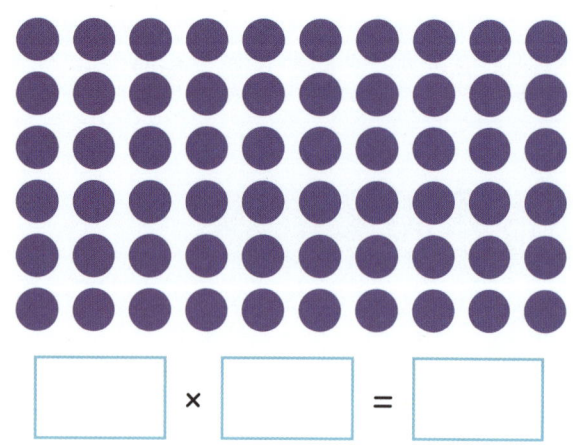

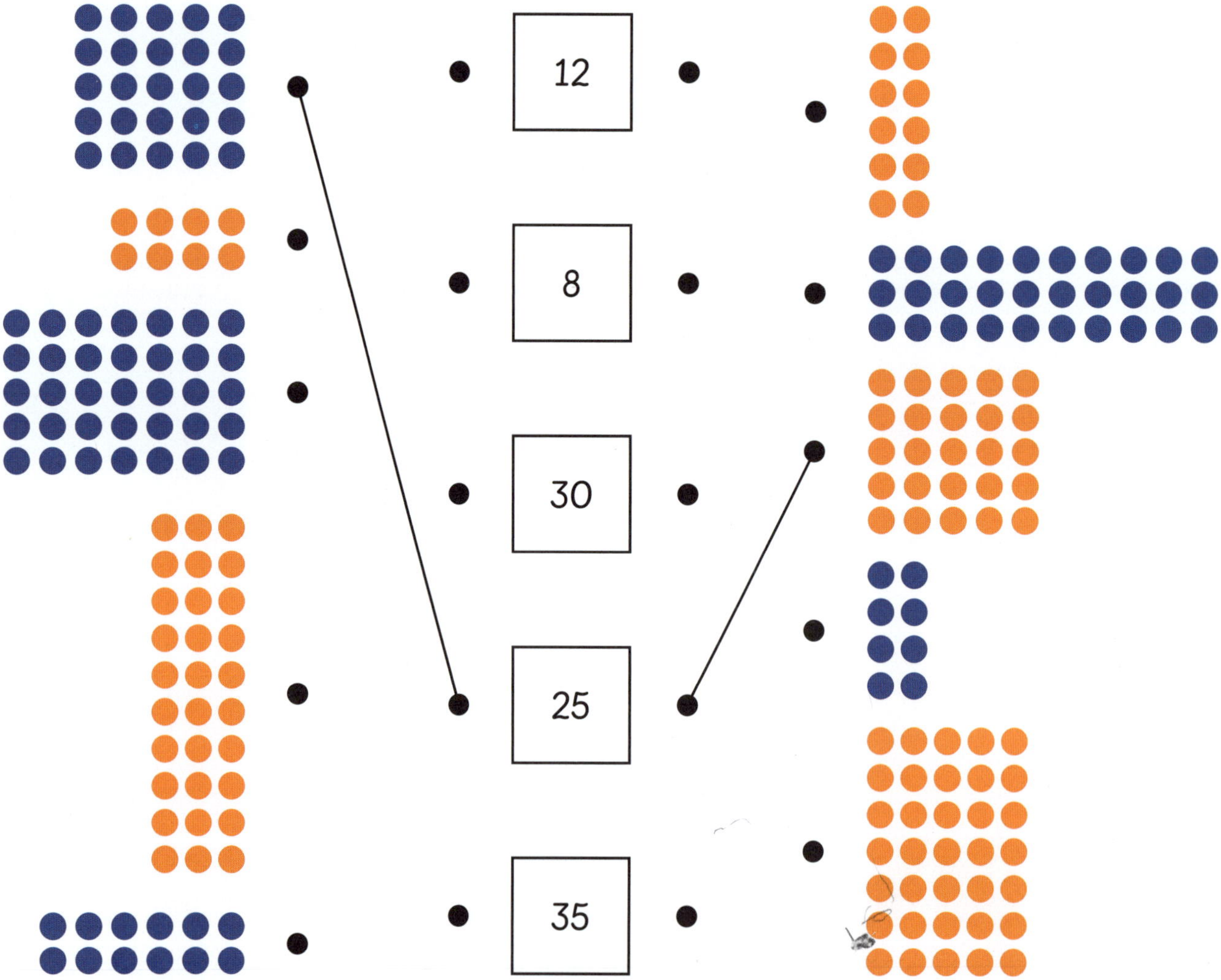

12

8

30

25

35

3 Write 2 equations for each picture.

(a)

☐ × ☐ = ☐

☐ × ☐ = ☐

(b)

☐ × ☐ = ☐

☐ × ☐ = ☐

(c)

☐ × ☐ = ☐

☐ × ☐ = ☐

Word Problems

Lesson 6

Starter

Sam prints 7 sheets of invitations for the school play.
Each sheet has 5 invitations.
How many invitations does Sam print?

Example

Sam prints 7 sheets.
Each sheet has 5 invitations.

$7 \times 5 = 35$

Sam prints 35 invitations.

Practice

Solve.

1 A farmer has 5 horses in his stable that need new horseshoes.
Each horse needs 4 horseshoes.
How many horseshoes does the farmer need?

2 10 children go the fair. Each child gets 8 ride tickets.
How many rides can the children take altogether?

3 An ice cream parlor sells 9 ice cream cones at lunchtime.
Each ice cream cone has 2 scoops of ice cream.
How many scoops of ice cream does the parlor use at lunchtime?

Grouping

Lesson 7

Starter

How many baskets of 5 apples can Hannah make?

Example

There are 30 apples in total. When I make groups of 5, I get 6 groups.
30 ÷ 5 = 6

÷ means to divide. 30 ÷ 5 = 6 is a division equation. We say 30 divided by 5 is equal to 6.

Hannah can make 6 baskets of 5 apples.

Practice

1 Circle to make groups of 5.
How many groups are there?

☐ ÷ ☐ = ☐

There are ☐ groups.

2 Circle to make groups of 2.
How many groups are there?

☐ ÷ ☐ = ☐

There are ☐ groups.

3 Fill in the blanks.

(a) Group the mugs in twos.

☐ ÷ ☐ = ☐

(b) Group the cupcakes in fives.

☐ ÷ ☐ = ☐

Sharing

Lesson 8

Starter

The game has 24 cards. I have to deal out all the cards equally.

How many cards does each player get?

Example

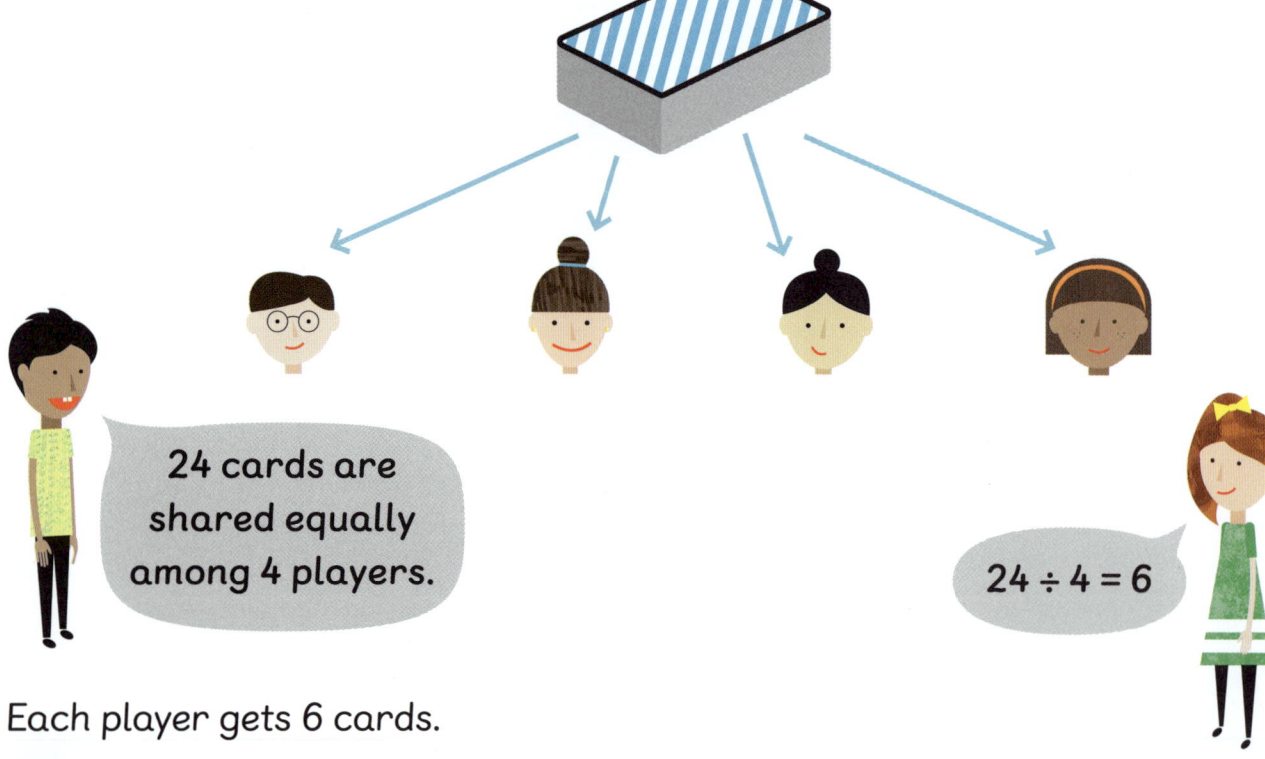

24 cards are shared equally among 4 players.

$24 \div 4 = 6$

Each player gets 6 cards.

Practice

Fill in the blanks.

1 Elliott has 12 doughnuts.

I put the doughnuts equally on 2 plates.

☐ ÷ ☐ = ☐

There are ☐ doughnuts on each plate.

2 Share 20 cards equally among 5 players.

☐ ÷ ☐ = ☐   5 × ☐ = ☐

3 Put 30 counters equally into 3 groups.

☐ ÷ ☐ = ☐   3 × ☐ = ☐

Dividing by 2

Lesson 9

Starter

Lulu needs to put the dice into groups of 2 for a game.
How many equal groups can Lulu make?

Example

18 ÷ 2 = 9
Lulu can make 9 equal groups.

I put 18 dice into groups of 2. I made 9 groups.

Practice

1 Sam puts the cookies into boxes.
Each box has 2 cookies.

☐ ÷ 2 = ☐

There are ☐ boxes of 2 cookies.

2 Ruby puts the grapes equally onto 2 plates.

☐ ÷ 2 = ☐

There are ☐ grapes on each plate.

3 Fill in the blanks.

(a) 8 ÷ 2 = ☐

(b) 16 ÷ 2 = ☐

(c) 20 ÷ 2 = ☐

(d) ☐ ÷ 2 = 5

Dividing by 5

Lesson 10

Starter

Jacob puts the colored pencils equally into 5 pots.
How many pencils does he put in each pot?

Example

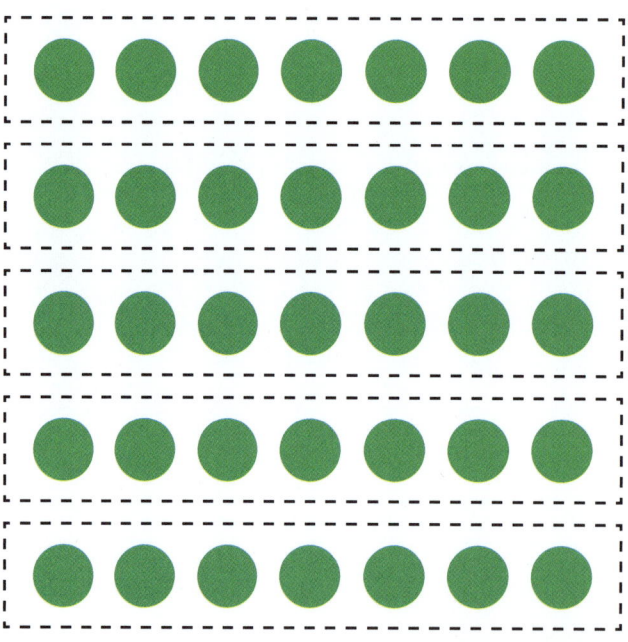

There are 35 pencils in total. There are 5 pots.

35 ÷ 5 = 7
Jacob puts 7 pencils in each pot.

Practice

1 Hannah puts the drinks into boxes. Each box has 5 drinks.

☐ ÷ 5 = ☐

There are ☐ boxes of 5 drinks.

2 Charles puts the slices of cake equally onto 5 plates.

☐ ÷ 5 = ☐

There are ☐ slices of cake on each plate.

3 Fill in the blanks.

(a) 20 ÷ 5 = ☐

(b) 50 ÷ 5 = ☐

(c) 35 ÷ 5 = ☐

(d) ☐ ÷ 5 = 5

Dividing by 10

Lesson 11

Starter

The chef has filled one box of chocolates so far.

How many more boxes can the chef fill?

Example

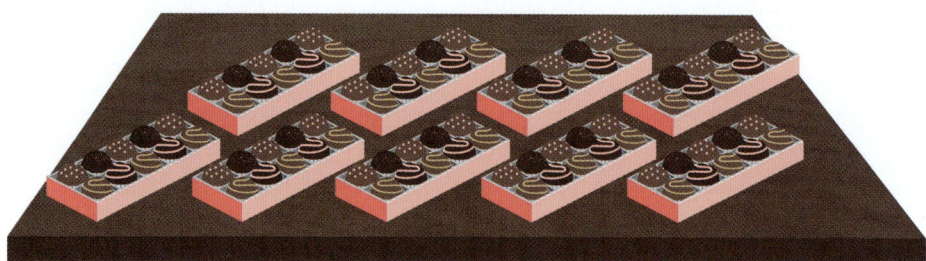

There are 90 chocolates left in the tray. Each box can hold 10 chocolates.
90 ÷ 10 = 9

The chef can fill 9 more boxes with chocolates.

Practice

1 Emma puts the counters into stacks.
Each stack has 10 counters.

☐ ÷ 10 = ☐

There are ☐ stacks of 10 counters.

2 Ravi puts the cookies equally onto 10 plates.

☐ ÷ 10 = ☐

There are ☐ cookies on each plate.

3 Fill in the blanks.

(a) 20 ÷ 10 = ☐   (b) 60 ÷ 10 = ☐

(c) ☐ ÷ 10 = 8   (d) ☐ ÷ 10 = 10

Multiplication and Division

Lesson 12

Starter

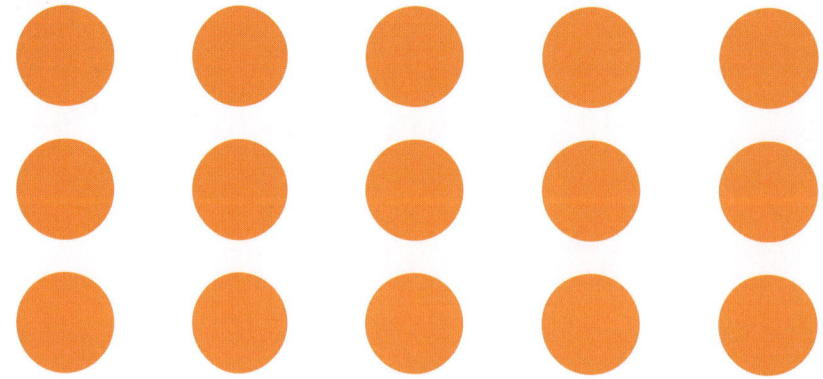

Can you write multiplication and division equations for this picture?

Example

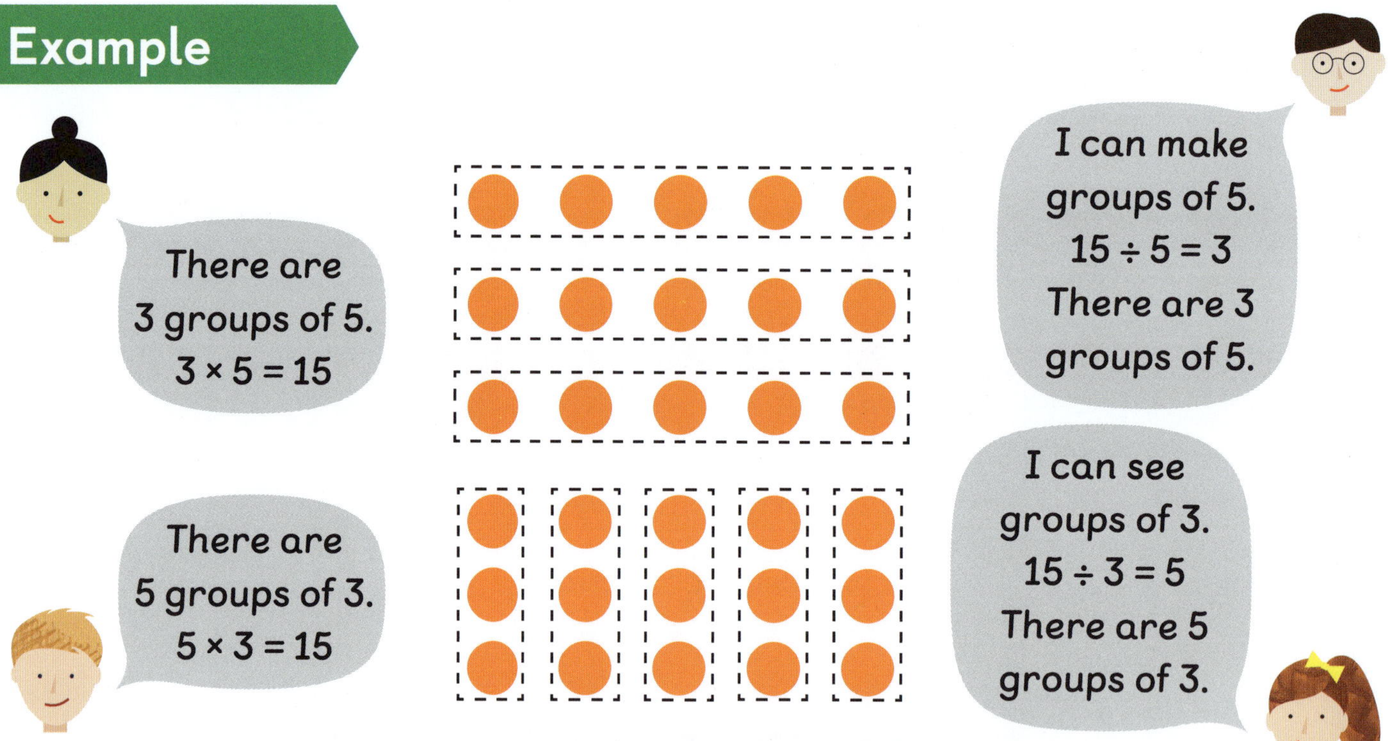

There are 3 groups of 5.
3 × 5 = 15

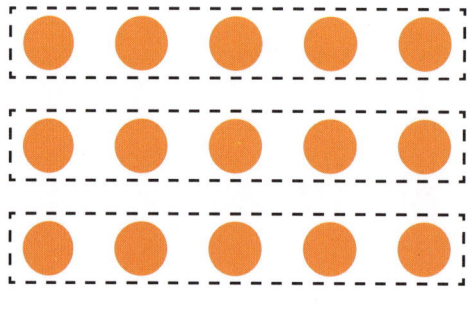

I can make groups of 5.
15 ÷ 5 = 3
There are 3 groups of 5.

There are 5 groups of 3.
5 × 3 = 15

I can see groups of 3.
15 ÷ 3 = 5
There are 5 groups of 3.

3 × 5 = 15   15 ÷ 5 = 3
5 × 3 = 15   15 ÷ 3 = 5

This is called a family of multiplication and division facts.

28

Practice

Complete the multiplication and division fact families.

1

2 × 4 = ☐   8 ÷ 4 = ☐

4 × 2 = ☐   8 ÷ 2 = ☐

2

3 × 4 = ☐   12 ÷ ☐ = 4

4 × 3 = ☐   ☐ ÷ 4 = ☐

3

☐ × ☐ = ☐   ☐ ÷ ☐ = ☐

☐ × ☐ = ☐   ☐ ÷ ☐ = ☐

More Word Problems

Lesson 13

Starter

Can the 3 children share the cookies equally?

Example

There are 15 cookies.
3 children share the cookies equally.
How many cookies does each child get?

Try Ravi's method to find how many cookies each child gets.

Ravi's method uses to stand for and to stand for each child.

Emma's method  draws a picture to show how many cookies each child gets.

Holly's method  uses a division equation.

15 ÷ 3 = 5

Each child gets 5 cookies.

Practice

1 Charles has 30 apples.
He wants to put the apples into bags.
Each bag should have 5 apples.
How many bags will he need?

Ravi's method

 uses to stand for and to stand for each bag.

Emma's method

 draws a picture to show how many bags Charles will need.

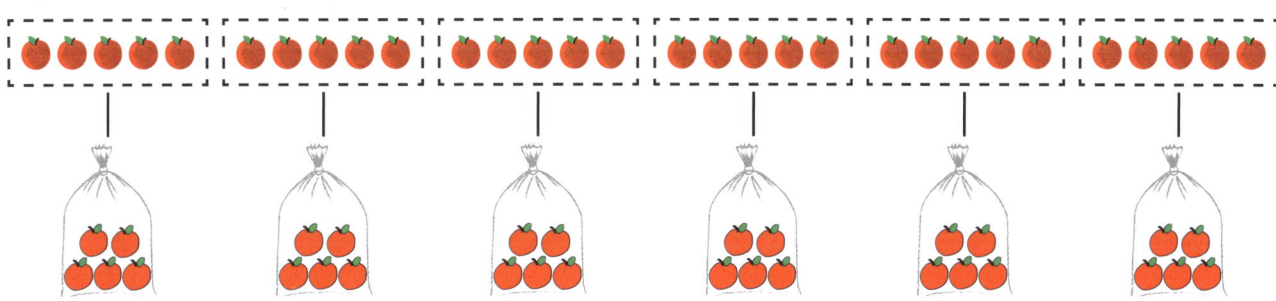

Holly's method

 uses a division equation.

☐ ÷ ☐ = ☐

Charles will need ☐ bags.

☐ × 5 = 30

2 The P. E. teacher has 12 soccer balls.
He gives some children 2 soccer balls each.
How many children get 2 soccer balls?

Ravi's method

 uses to stand for and 🥤 to stand for each child.

Emma's method

 draws a picture to show how many children get 2 soccer balls.

Holly's method

 uses a division equation.

☐ ÷ ☐ = ☐

☐ children get 2 soccer balls.

☐ × 2 = 12

3 Solve and fill in the blanks.

(a) Elliott and Ravi make 16 paper planes.
They share them equally.
How many paper planes does each of them get?

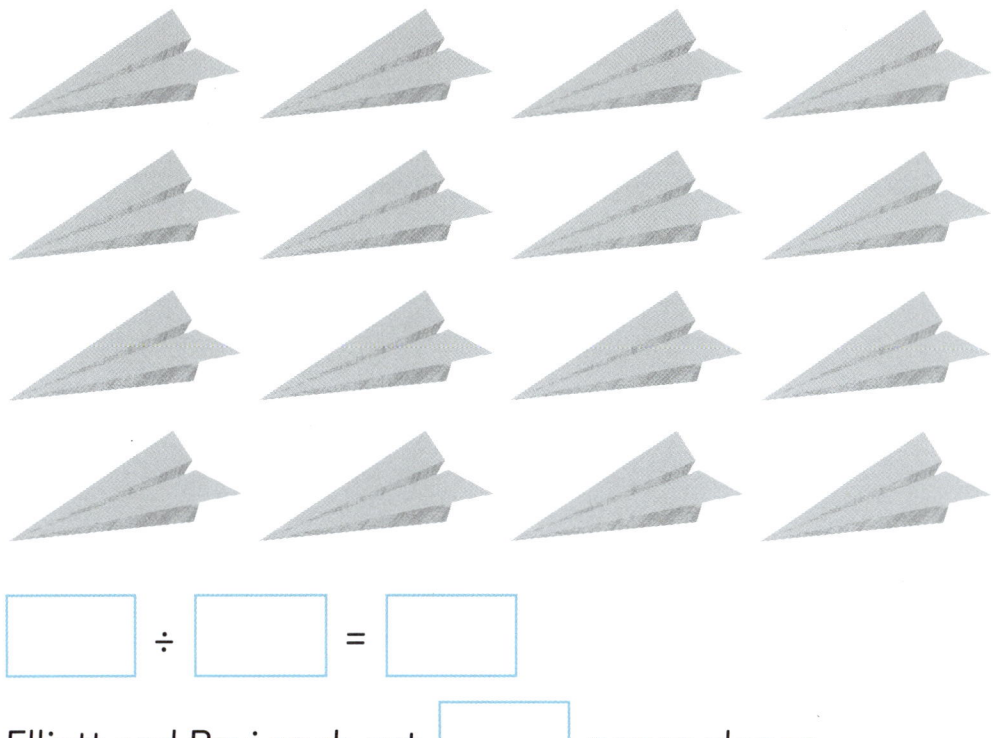

☐ ÷ ☐ = ☐

Elliott and Ravi each get ☐ paper planes.

(b) A baker has 100 muffins. She puts them into boxes of 10.
How many boxes does she fill?

☐ ÷ ☐ = ☐

The baker fills ☐ boxes.

(c) Amira has 35 magnets.
She places them equally into 7 boxes.
How many magnets does she place in each box?

☐ ÷ ☐ = ☐

Amira places ☐ magnets in each box.

(d) There are 60 children in the gym.
They are sitting in groups of 6.
How many groups of children are there in the gym?

☐ ÷ ☐ = ☐

There are ☐ groups of children in the gym.

4 Solve and fill in the blanks.

Jacob has 20 apples.

He wants to place them equally on some plates.

(a) How many plates would he need if he places 2 apples on each plate?

☐ ÷ ☐ = ☐

He would need ☐ plates.

(b) How many plates would he need if he places 5 apples on each plate?

☐ ÷ ☐ = ☐

He would need ☐ plates.

(c) How many plates would he need if he places 10 apples on each plate?

☐ ÷ ☐ = ☐

He would need ☐ plates.

There is more than one way to arrange the apples in equal groups.

Review and Challenge

1 Fill in the blanks.

☐ + ☐ + ☐ + ☐ + ☐ + ☐ = ☐

☐ groups of ☐ = ☐

☐ × ☐ = ☐

2 Fill in the blanks.

(a) 1 × 2 = ☐

(b) 2 × 2 = ☐

(c) 2 × 5 = ☐

(d) 5 × 6 = ☐

(e) 10 × 2 = ☐

(f) 2 × 7 = ☐

(g) 7 × 2 = ☐

(h) 8 × 2 = ☐

(i) 5 × 5 = ☐

(j) 8 × 10 = ☐

3 Count in fives and highlight the numbers on the number chart. The first one is done for you.

1	2	3	4	5	6	7	8	9	10
11	12	13	14	15	16	17	18	19	20
21	22	23	24	25	26	27	28	29	30
31	32	33	34	35	36	37	38	39	40
41	42	43	44	45	46	47	48	49	50

4 Count in tens and highlight the numbers on the number chart.

1	2	3	4	5	6	7	8	9	10
11	12	13	14	15	16	17	18	19	20
21	22	23	24	25	26	27	28	29	30
31	32	33	34	35	36	37	38	39	40
41	42	43	44	45	46	47	48	49	50
51	52	53	54	55	56	57	58	59	60
61	62	63	64	65	66	67	68	69	70
71	72	73	74	75	76	77	78	79	80
81	82	83	84	85	86	87	88	89	90
91	92	93	94	95	96	97	98	99	100

5 Fill in the blanks.

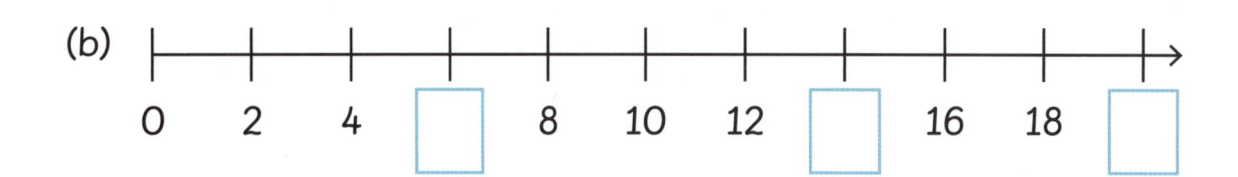

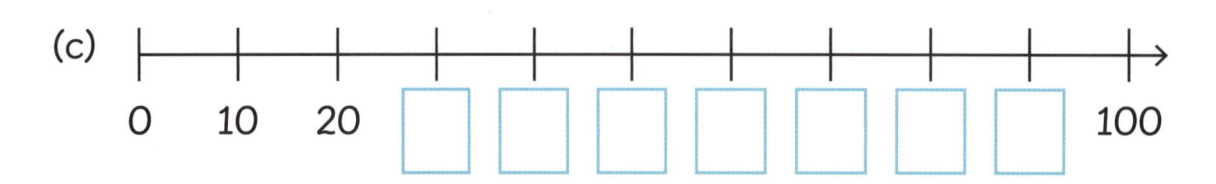

(a) 0, 5, ☐, 15, 20, ☐, ☐, ☐, ☐, 45, ☐

(b) 0, 2, 4, ☐, 8, 10, 12, ☐, 16, 18, ☐

(c) 0, 10, 20, ☐, ☐, ☐, ☐, ☐, ☐, ☐, 100

6 Fill in the blanks.

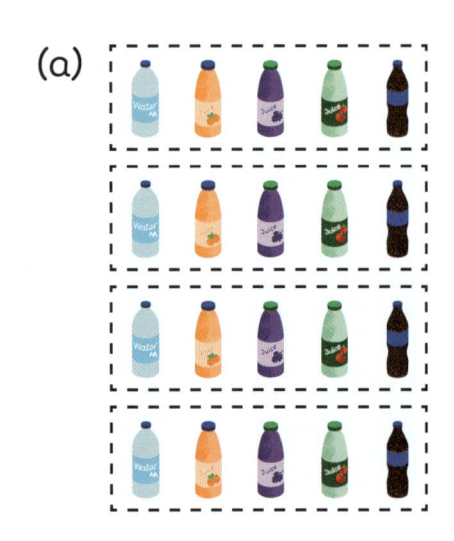

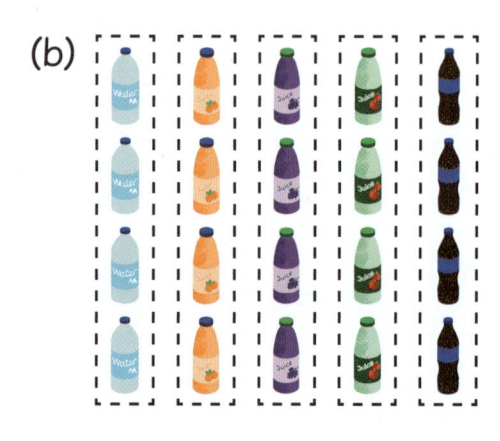

(a)

(b)

☐ groups of ☐ = ☐

☐ × ☐ = ☐

☐ groups of ☐ = ☐

☐ × ☐ = ☐

7 Fill in the blanks.

(a)

2 × ☐ = ☐ × 2

(b)

☐ × ☐ = ☐ × ☐

8 Fill in the blanks. Draw pictures to help you.

(a) A florist has 6 vases. He puts 5 flowers in each vase. How many flowers does he put in the vases in total?

☐ × ☐ = ☐

The florist puts ☐ in the vases in total.

(b) Oak has 3 baskets. She places 10 bowls in each basket. How many bowls are there altogether?

☐ × ☐ = ☐

There are ☐ bowls altogether.

9 Solve and fill in the blanks.
Lulu and her friends are playing a game.

Lulu shares 50 playing cards with her friends.
How many cards does each friend get?

[ ] ÷ [ ] = [ ]

Each friend gets [ ] playing cards.

10 Solve and fill in the blanks.
Jacob needs to fill baskets with 5 lemons each.
He has 45 lemons.
How many baskets can he fill?

45 lemons

[ ] ÷ [ ] = [ ]

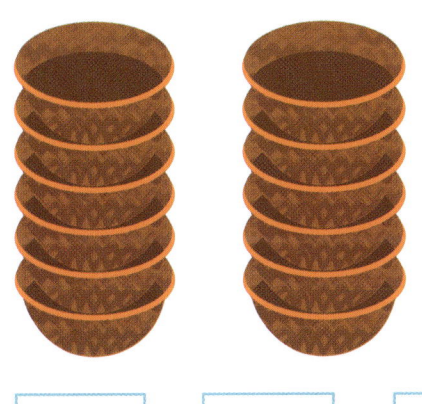

Jacob can fill [ ] baskets.

11 Fill in the blanks.

(a) 30 ÷ 5 = ☐   (b) 30 ÷ 10 = ☐

(c) 8 ÷ 2 = ☐   (d) 90 ÷ 10 = ☐

(e) 10 ÷ 5 = ☐   (f) 10 ÷ 2 = ☐

(g) 35 ÷ 5 = ☐   (h) 100 ÷ 10 = ☐

12 Complete the multiplication and division fact families.

5 × 4 = ☐   20 ÷ ☐ = 4

4 × 5 = ☐   ☐ ÷ 4 = ☐

13 Complete the multiplication and division fact families.

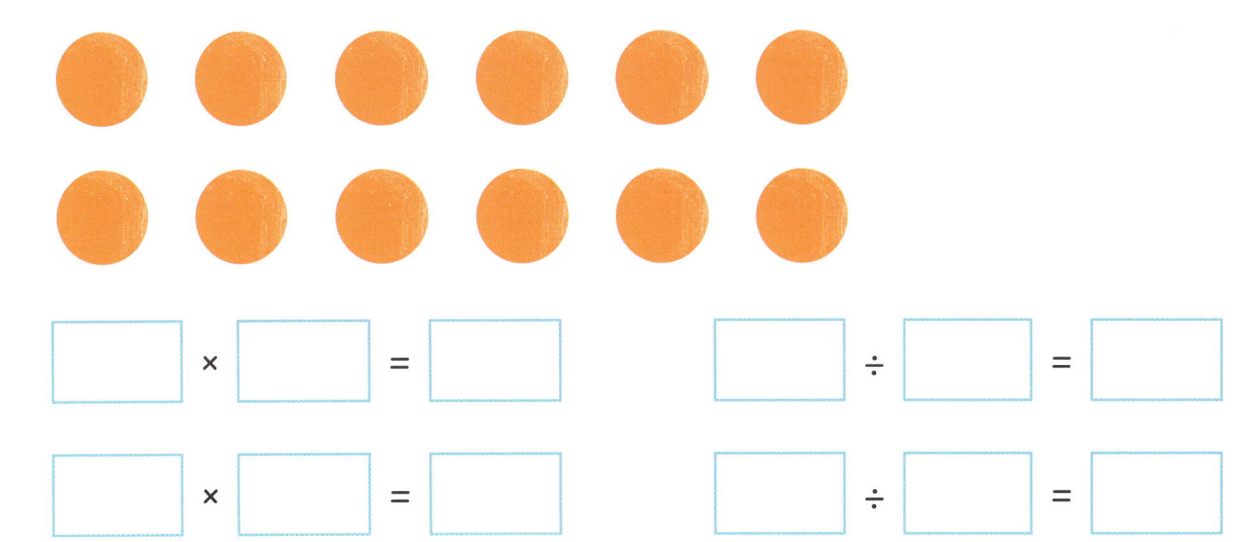

● ● ● ● ● ●
● ● ● ● ● ●

☐ × ☐ = ☐   ☐ ÷ ☐ = ☐

☐ × ☐ = ☐   ☐ ÷ ☐ = ☐

14 Solve and fill in the blanks.

(a) Emma and her mom need to make 60 muffins for the school bake sale.
They can bake 10 muffins in one batch.
How many batches do they need to bake?

☐ ÷ ☐ = ☐

They need to bake ☐ batches.

(b) Sam wants to place 45 books equally on 5 shelves.
How many books should he place on each shelf?

☐ ÷ ☐ = ☐

He should place ☐ books on each shelf.

15 Ravi has 40 counters. He wants to arrange them into equal rows.

The diagram below shows one way Ravi can do this.

Draw to show different ways Ravi can arrange the counters.

Fill in the blanks to show the multiplication and subtraction fact families.

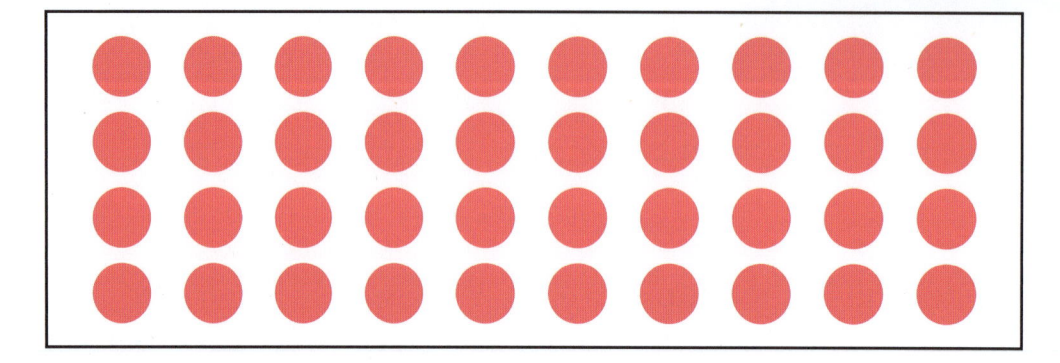

☐ × ☐ = ☐   ☐ ÷ ☐ = ☐

☐ × ☐ = ☐   ☐ ÷ ☐ = ☐

☐ × ☐ = ☐   ☐ ÷ ☐ = ☐

☐ × ☐ = ☐   ☐ ÷ ☐ = ☐

[ ] × [ ] = [ ]   [ ] ÷ [ ] = [ ]

[ ] × [ ] = [ ]   [ ] ÷ [ ] = [ ]

16 Oak has 3 packs of 10 baseball cards. She buys another 4 packs of 10 baseball cards. She then gives 2 packs to Jacob.

Oak gives Jacob [ ] cards.

She has [ ] cards left.

17 Sam drew the invitations for the school concert so that 10 invitations can fit on each sheet of paper. He needs 35 invitations for the families and 15 invitations for the teachers.
How many sheets of invitations does Sam need to print?

Sam needs to print [ ] sheets of invitations.

Answers

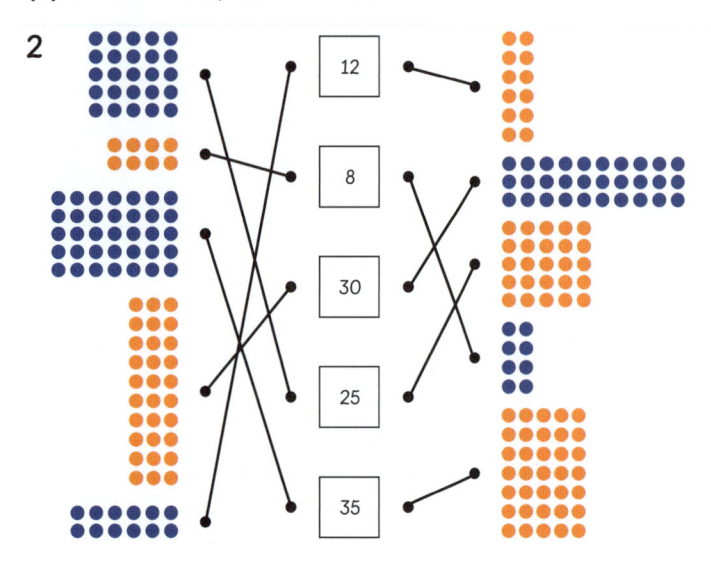

Page 5
1 5 + 5 + 5 = 15, 3 groups of 5 = 15, 3 × 5 = 15
2 5 + 5 + 5 + 5 + 5 + 5 = 30, 6 groups of 5 = 30, 6 × 5 = 30

Page 7
2 × 2 = 4, 3 groups of 2 = 6, 3 × 2 = 6, 4 groups of 2 = 8, 4 × 2 = 8, 5 groups of 2 = 10, 5 × 2 = 10, 6 groups of 2 = 12, 6 × 2 = 12, 7 groups of 2 = 14, 7 × 2 = 14, 8 groups of 2 = 16, 8 × 2 = 16, 9 groups of 2 = 18, 9 × 2 = 18, 10 groups of 2 = 20, 10 × 2 = 20

Page 9
2 × 5 = 10, 3 groups of 5 = 15, 3 × 5 = 15, 4 groups of 5 = 20, 4 × 5 = 20, 5 groups of 5 = 25, 5 × 5 = 25, 6 groups of 5 = 30, 6 × 5 = 30, 7 groups of 5 = 35, 7 × 5 = 35, 8 groups of 5 = 40, 8 × 5 = 40, 9 groups of 5 = 45, 9 × 5 = 45, 10 groups of 5 = 50, 10 × 5 = 50

Page 11
1 (a) 4 groups of 10 = 40, 4 × 10 = 40 **(b)** 3 groups of 10 = 30, 3 × 10 = 30
(c) 7 groups of 10 = 70, 7 × 10 = 70 **2 (a)** 20 **(b)** 60 **(c)** 50 **(d)** 100

Page 13
1 (a) 5 × 3 = 3 × 5, 5 × 3 = 15, 3 × 5 = 15 **(b)** 2 × 4 = 8, 4 × 2 = 8

Page 14
(c) 6 × 10 = 60, 10 × 6 = 60

Page 15
3 (a) 4 × 5 = 20, 5 × 4 = 20 **(b)** 8 × 5 = 40, 5 × 8 = 40 **(c)** 2 × 6 = 12, 6 × 2 = 12

Page 17
1 5 × 4 = 20. The farmer needs 20 horseshoes. **2** 10 × 8 = 80. The children can take 80 rides altogether. **3** 9 × 2 = 18. The parlor uses 18 scoops of ice cream at lunchtime.

Page 19
1 15 ÷ 5 = 3. There are 3 groups. **2** 8 ÷ 2 = 4. There are 4 groups. **3 (a)** 6 ÷ 2 = 3
(b) 20 ÷ 5 = 4

Page 21
1 12 ÷ 2 = 6. There are 6 doughnuts on each plate. **2** 20 ÷ 5 = 4, 5 × 4 = 20 **3** 30 ÷ 3 = 10, 3 × 10 = 30

Page 23
1 20 ÷ 2 = 10. There are 10 boxes of 2 cookies. **2** 16 ÷ 2 = 8. There are 8 grapes on each plate. **3 (a)** 4 **(b)** 8 **(c)** 10 **(d)** 10

46

Page 25   **1** 20 ÷ 5 = 4. There are 4 boxes of 5 drinks.   **2** 10 ÷ 5 = 2. There are 2 slices of cake on each plate.   **3 (a)** 4   **(b)** 10   **(c)** 7   **(d)** 25

Page 27   **1** 40 ÷ 10 = 4. There are 4 stacks of 10 counters.   **2** 30 ÷ 10 = 3. There are 3 cookies on each plate.   **3 (a)** 2   **(b)** 6   **(c)** 80   **(d)** 100

Page 29   **1** 2 × 4 = 8, 8 ÷ 4 = 2, 4 × 2 = 8, 8 ÷ 2 = 4   **2** 3 × 4 = 12, 12 ÷ 3 = 4, 4 × 3 = 12, 12 ÷ 4 = 3   **3** 2 × 5 = 10, 10 ÷ 5 = 2, 5 × 2 = 10, 10 ÷ 2 = 5

Page 31   **1** 30 ÷ 5 = 6. Charles will need 6 bags. 6 × 5 = 30

Page 32   **2** 12 ÷ 2 = 6. 6 children get 2 soccer balls. 6 × 2 = 12

Page 33   **3 (a)** 16 ÷ 2 = 8. Elliott and Ravi each get 8 paper planes.   **(b)** 100 ÷ 10 = 10. The baker fills 10 boxes.

Page 34   **(c)** 35 ÷ 7 = 5. Amira places 5 magnets in each box.   **(d)** 60 ÷ 6 = 10. There are 10 groups of children in the gym.

Page 35   **4 (a)** 20 ÷ 2 = 10. He would need 10 plates.   **(b)** 20 ÷ 5 = 4. He would need 4 plates.   **(c)** 20 ÷ 10 = 2. He would need 2 plates.

Page 36   **1** 5 + 5 + 5 + 5 + 5 + 5 = 30, 6 groups of 5 = 30, 6 × 5 = 30   **2 (a)** 2   **(b)** 4   **(c)** 10   **(d)** 30   **(e)** 20   **(f)** 14   **(g)** 14   **(h)** 16   **(i)** 25   **(j)** 80

Page 37   **3**

1	2	3	4	5	6	7	8	9	10
11	12	13	14	15	16	17	18	19	20
21	22	23	24	25	26	27	28	29	30
31	32	33	34	35	36	37	38	39	40
41	42	43	44	45	46	47	48	49	50

4

1	2	3	4	5	6	7	8	9	10
11	12	13	14	15	16	17	18	19	20
21	22	23	24	25	26	27	28	29	30
31	32	33	34	35	36	37	38	39	40
41	42	43	44	45	46	47	48	49	50
51	52	53	54	55	56	57	58	59	60
61	62	63	64	65	66	67	68	69	70
71	72	73	74	75	76	77	78	79	80
81	82	83	84	85	86	87	88	89	90
91	92	93	94	95	96	97	98	99	100

Page 38   **5 (a)** 10, 25, 30, 35, 40, 50   **(b)** 6, 14, 20   **(c)** 30, 40, 50, 60, 70, 80, 90   **6 (a)** 4 groups of 5 = 20, 4 × 5 = 20   **(b)** 5 groups of 4 = 20, 5 × 4 = 20

Page 39   **7 (a)** 2 × 4 = 4 × 2   **(b)** 6 × 10 = 10 × 6

Page 40   **8 (a)** 6 × 5 = 30. He puts 30 flowers in the vases in total.   **(b)** 3 × 10 = 30. There are 30 bowls altogether.

Page 41   **9** 50 ÷ 5 = 10. Each friend gets 10 playing cards.   **10** 45 ÷ 5 = 9. Jacob can fill 9 baskets.

Page 42   **11 (a)** 6   **(b)** 3   **(c)** 4   **(d)** 9   **(e)** 2   **(f)** 5   **(g)** 7   **(h)** 10   **12** 5 × 4 = 20, 20 ÷ 5 = 4, 4 × 5 = 20, 20 ÷ 4 = 5

Page 43   **13 (a)** 6 × 2 = 12, 12 ÷ 6 = 2, 2 × 6 = 12, 12 ÷ 2 = 6   **14 (a)** 60 ÷ 10 = 6. They need to bake 6 batches.   **(b)** 45 ÷ 5 = 9. He should place 9 books on each shelf.

Answers continued

Page 44–45   **15** 10 × 4 = 40, 4 × 10 = 40, 40 ÷ 4 = 10, 40 ÷ 10 = 4
Possible answers include: 8 × 5 = 40, 5 × 8 = 40, 40 ÷ 5 = 8, 40 ÷ 8 = 5
The next family of equations as follows: 20 × 2 = 40, 2 × 20 = 40, 40 ÷ 2 = 20, 40 ÷ 20 = 2
40 × 1 = 40, 1 × 40 = 40, 40 ÷ 1 = 40, 40 ÷ 40 = 1

Page 45   **16** Oak gives Jacob 20 cards. She has 50 cards left.   **17** Sam needs to print 5 sheets of invitations.